For Mom from a Thankful Heart
Copyright 1999 by ZondervanPublishingHouse

ISBN 0-310-97962-5

Published under license from ZondervanPublishingHouse

Printed in China

99 00 01 02 03 / HK / 12 11 10 9 8 7 6 5 4

for

Mom

From a
Thankful Heart

Hallmark
BOOKS

 Zondervan

BOK4017

Behold, children are a gift of the LORD; the fruit of the womb is a reward.

PSALM 127:3
NASB

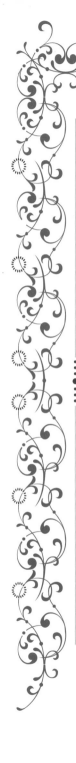

Lord,
 in this frenzied puttering
 about the house,
 see more!
The dusting,
 straightening,
 muttering
 are but the poor
 efforts of a heavy heart
 to help time pass.
Praying on my knees
 I get uptight;
 for hearts and lives
 are not the only things
 that need to be
 put right.
And, while I clean,
 please,
 if tears should fall,
 they're settling the dust,
 —that's all.
Lord,
 I will straighten all I can
 and You
 take over what we mothers
 cannot do.

RUTH BELL GRAHAM

They say that man is mighty,
  He governs land and sea,
He wields a mighty scepter
O'er lesser powers that be;
But a mightier power and stronger
Man from his throne has hurled,
For the hand that rocks the cradle
Is the hand that rules the world.

WILLIAM ROSS WALLACE

His praise shall continually be in my mouth.

Continually?
Yes! We can say with the Psalm writer:

"O LORD, open my lips,
and my mouth will declare
your praise."

Psalm 51:15

Sometimes
praising God
seems more than I can do!

I don't feel full of praise
when the dentist is drilling
or the children are fighting
or the doctor is probing;
when there's been an accident
or the washer overflows
or my head is pounding . . .

Screaming? Yes.
Crying? Maybe.
But praising?

But are those the very times I should praise you?
Would praise put the incident in perspective
and free my mind to hear you speak?

Don't let me wait until I understand . . .
Just help me praise now
and learn later.

MARGARET B. SPIESS

*A*s moms, we go from a free existence to the beck and call of a bundle weighing scarcely more than a well-stocked purse. And then, as soon as we adjust to losing our lives to another, our little ones decide they need our help less than we want to give it. "I can do it myself!" replaces their squawking insistence that we do it for them.

Change is rough. How do we react to our little ones launching off our laps? To the school bus? To two weeks away at summer camp? To an apartment of their own, a relationship, a marriage?

We grieve for what is no more, turn our children over to God and rejoice in what he has created in them. And we check the mailbox every day for two weeks for a letter from camp.

ELISA MORGAN

Adam named his wife Eve ["Eve" probably means "living"], because she would become the mother of all the living.

GENESIS 3:20
NIV

Five I have:
  each separate,
distinct,
a soul
bound for eternity:
and I
—blind
leader of the blind—
groping and fumbling,
casual and concerned,
by turns . . .
undisciplined, I seek
by order and command
to discipline and shape;
(I who need
Thy discipline
to shape
my own disordered soul.)
O Thou
Who seest the heart's
true, deep desire,
each shortcoming and
each sad mistake,
supplement
and
overrule,
nor let our children be
the victims of our own
unlikeness unto Thee.

RUTH BELL GRAHAM

The Christian mother must turn a deaf ear to the babble of voices vying for her attention and listen to God. It is in Scripture that she will find the only safe and reliable information about how to fulfill her calling as a wife and mother.

BARBARA BUSH

At that time Mary got
ready and hurried to a town in the hill country
of Judea, where she entered Zechariah's home
and greeted Elizabeth. When Elizabeth heard
Mary's greeting, the baby leaped in her womb,
and Elizabeth was filled with the Holy Spirit.
In a loud voice she exclaimed: "Blessed are you
among women, and blessed is the child you will
bear! But why am I so favored, that the mother
of my Lord should come to me? As soon as the
sound of your greeting reached my ears, the
baby in my womb leaped for joy. Blessed is she
who has believed that what the Lord has said to
her will be accomplished!"

And Mary said:

"My soul glorifies the Lord
and my spirit rejoices in God my Savior,
for he has been mindful
of the humble state of his servant.
From now on all generations will call me
blessed,
for the Mighty One has done great things
for me—
holy is his name.
His mercy extends to those who fear him,
from generation to generation.
He has performed mighty deeds with his
arm;
he has scattered those who are proud in
their inmost thoughts.
He has brought down rulers from their
thrones
but has lifted up the humble.
He has filled the hungry with good things
but has sent the rich away empty.
He has helped his servant Israel,
remembering to be merciful
to Abraham and his descendants forever,
even as he said to our fathers."

LUKE 1:39-55

NIV

WHAT CHILD IS THIS?
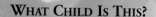

What child is this, who, laid to
rest, On Mary's lap is sleeping?
Whom angels greet with anthems sweet,
While shepherds watch are keeping?
This, this is Christ the King,
Whom shepherds guard and angels sing;
Haste, haste to bring Him laud,
The babe, the son of Mary.

This is how the birth of Jesus Christ came about: His mother Mary was pledged to be married to Joseph, but before they came together, she was found to be with child through the Holy Spirit. Because Joseph her husband was a righteous man and did not want to expose her to public disgrace, he had in mind to divorce her quietly.

But after he had considered this, an angel of the Lord appeared to him in a dream and said, "Joseph son of David, do not be afraid to take Mary home as your wife, because what is conceived in her is from the Holy Spirit. She will give birth to a son, and you are to give him the name Jesus, because he will save his people from their sins."

MATTHEW 1:18-21

NIV

We have forgotten the mystery, the dimension of glory. It was Mary herself who showed it to us so plainly. By the offering up of her physical body to become the God-bearer, she transfigured for all mothers, for all time, the meaning of motherhood. She cradled, fed and bathed her baby—who was very God of very God—so that when we cradle, feed and bathe ours we may see beyond that simple task to the God who in love and humility "dwelt among us and we beheld his glory."

Those who focus only on the drabness of the supermarket, or on the onions or the diapers themselves, haven't an inkling of the mystery that is at stake here, the mystery revealed in the birth of that Baby and consummated on the Cross: my life for yours.

The routines of housework and of mothering may be seen as a kind of death, and it is appropriate that they should be, for they offer the chance, day after day, to lay down one's life for others. Then they are no longer routines. . . . A mother's part in sustaining the life of her children and making it pleasant and comfortable is no triviality. It calls for self-sacrifice and humility, but it is the route, as was the humiliation of Jesus, to glory.

ELISABETH ELLIOT

*Y*ou may have tangible
wealth untold,
Caskets of jewels
and coffers of gold.
Richer than I you can never be—
I had a mother who read to me.

STRICKLAND GILLIAN

Rock Me to Sleep

*B*ackward, turn backward, O Time,
   in your flight,
Make me a child again just for tonight!
Mother, come back from the echoless shore,
Take me again to your heart as of yore;
   Kiss from my forehead the furrows
     of care,
   Smooth the few silver threads out
     of my hair;
   Over my slumbers your loving
     watch keep;
   Rock me to sleep, Mother, rock
     me to sleep.
   Over my heart in the days
     that are flown,
No love like mother-love ever has shone;
No other worship abides and endures,
Faithful, unselfish, and patient like yours:
None like a mother can charm away pain
From the sick soul and the world-weary brain.
Slumber's soft calms o'er my heavy lids creep;
Rock me to sleep, Mother, rock me to sleep!

ELIZABETH AKERS ALLEN

*May you live
to see your
children's
children.*

PSALM 128:6
NIV

I've often wondered why the law requires that we have a license to drive a car, catch fish, cut hair, and polish finger-nails—but we don't need a license to become a mother. It's reassuring to know that although the job is bigger than I can ever handle alone, I don't have to do it alone. God is with me every step of the way.

KATHY PEEL

*O*ne of the blessings of faith in Christ is that we recognize that raising our kids isn't all up to us. We need the security of knowing Christ and of being able to spend time with Him on a regular basis, praying and reading His Word. His principles are timeless. They alone last through all social changes. They are applicable in every situation. And they provide us with a foundation upon which to raise our families. A vital relationship with Christ is like the rudder of the ship that keeps individuals and families on course no matter what the weather.

SUSAN ALEXANDER YATES

*W*ho is like the LORD
our God, the One who sits enthroned on high,
who stoops down to look
on the heavens and the earth?
He raises the poor from the dust
and lifts the needy from the ash heap;
he seats them with princes,
with the princes of their people.
He settles the barren woman in her home
as a happy mother of children.
Praise the LORD.

PSALM 113:5-9
NIV

I have been reminded
of your [Timothy's] sincere faith, which first
lived in your grandmother Lois and in your
mother Eunice and, I am persuaded, now lives
in you also.

2 TIMOTHY 1:5
NIV

*A*t the end of your life, you'll never regret not having passed one more test, not winning one more verdict, or not closing one more deal. You will regret times not spent with a husband, a friend, a child, or a parent.

BARBARA BUSH

*Speech to 1990 Graduating Class
of Wellesley College*

Mom was left with three young children to care for when my father died at age thirty-three. I was seven years old at the time and had two younger brothers—ages five and two. Mom had not worked outside her home since she was married.

For the next six-and-a half years Mom was a single parent. I can remember how she made do with what she had so that she could give us the best possible childhood. Twice each week during those six summers she would take the three of us swimming and picnicking. All year long she would buy fabrics on sale and then sew clothes for us for Christmas gifts. I remember coming down for a drink of water late one night. There she was, busily sewing flannel pajamas for my brothers. She also sewed doll clothes so I could have something new to get excited about.

Mom had a small pension from my dad's service in World War II. To supplement her income she cleaned other people's homes. The money she earned helped to keep us in Christian school. Mom remarried when I was almost fourteen. She even had another child, so I finally had a sister.

Now that I'm an adult with my own grown children, I can finally appreciate what Mom went through with few material goods and a lot of loneliness in her life. I really appreciate her dedication to giving us the best life she could.

SHARON COELING

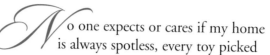

*N*o one expects or cares if my home is always spotless, every toy picked up, every table shining like the wax commercials. What they do care about, what they do notice, is if there is warmth and love in the home. If I am honest, I have to admit that many of the expectations and demands

are from no one but myself— not from my husband, not from my family, not from my friends, and certainly not from the Lord Jesus.

GIGI GRAHAM TCHIVIDJIAN

*E*veryone else is asleep after a
	long day
while I,
tired
cross
and unwilling,
am doing the dishes.
At this hour
throwing them out the window
has definite appeal!
Help me find some way to get through.

As I wash these dishes
let me wash my mind
of the day's annoyances
disappointments
failures . . .
but the good times must not drain away.
Help me sort them out,
treasure them
like panning gold.

Instead of the cross salesgirl,
let me remember my son's laughter;
instead of the missed appointment,
the letter from a friend.
Sometimes the nuggets are small,
the panning tedious,
but each day has gold for me to garner . . .
make me a miser, Lord!

MARGARET B. SPIESS

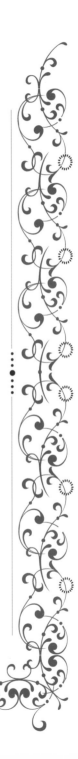

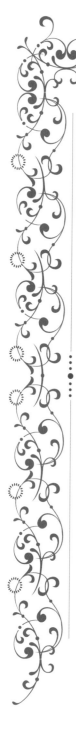

"Don't ever become so busy that you fail to realize how very happy you are!"

Mother's statement has meant much to me as I have raised our family. Whenever I have felt overly busy to the point of neglecting the little joys, the expressions of appreciation, the realization of how happy we are—whenever play with the children seemed more of a duty than a privilege, I have thought of Mother's words. They have been a warning beacon that has changed my attitude toward life and toward what is valuable.

KATHRYN HILLEN

Two things cannot alter,
  Since time was, nor today;
The flowing of water;
And love's strange, sweet way.

AUTHOR UNKNOWN

*K*nowing that God accepts us simply because we are His gives us security. Understanding that there is total acceptance of us by our families because we are family will create an atmosphere of approval and a sense of family identity.

A home whose atmosphere is marked by the ingredient of love will be a home where the members sense acceptance from one another, a home where they return to be filled up to go out into the world.

SUSAN ALEXANDER YATES

*O*ur deep need to be assured that someone really understands us, to share our innermost feelings with another, is not silly. It is a yearning built into our natures by God at creation. . . . It is essential, then, for us to know that we are not on our own as mothers without a divine hand to guide us or a source of wisdom to which to turn. The God who understands each of us completely as a person is also our everlasting Father and the Master of every skill needed for godly motherhood.

BARBARA BUSH

I love being a mother because my children allow me to lavish them with love. All I give them, they happily receive and enjoy. They have blessed me, prayed for me, thanked me, appreciated me, and, of course, I'm then encouraged to give more love.

MARIE CHAPIAN

My mother is the ultimate trivia buff. She collects interesting tidbits like some people collect stamps. She reads anything she can get her hands on and then parcels out her knowledge to the rest of the family.

Mom taught me a lot through the things she said, but she taught me even more through the things she did. Her example taught me more about compassion and kindness than anything she could have imparted to me in words.

I watched her as she invited friends into our home to study the Bible. Many of them came to the Lord around our kitchen table.

I watched as she spent whole days caring for our elderly neighbor who was dying of cancer. I watched as she sacrificed her well-deserved free days to home-school my brother and me for four years. In countless ways, both small and large, she showed me what it meant to love others.

I'm thankful for Mom's love of trivia and knowledge. Her passion for learning was contagious, and she passed it on to me. I'm even more thankful for her love for people. Through her example I was able to see the power of God's love flowing through human hands.

> *The heart of a mother is a deep abyss at the bottom of which you will always find forgiveness.*
>
> **HONÓRE DE BALZAC**

MOLLY DETWEILER

I had a friend who kept the messiest house in town, rarely got a meal together on time, ironed what clothes the children needed right before the school bus came. While maintaining better control than that is important to me, it wasn't to her. Every day when the kids got home, she sat and leisurely listened to their chatter. With four children this could take hours! All this "time-killing" made me nervous, but in the long run I learned a valuable lesson from her. The art of communication takes time and when the children feel they are worth it, the atmosphere is set at "secure."

The atmosphere of the home has nothing to do with décor or style. Rather, for the family it's a lot more than that. It's a feeling of being wanted and cared for. It's the smell of something simmering in a pot or baking in an oven. It's knowing Mom has time for listening and really being interested in how school was. It's a welcome mat for friends. It's a home that's reasonably clean but not sterile and untouchable.

For me it means that I've gotten most of my personal daily goals out of the way so my children understand they are the most important people I know. I have failed so often at this I am ashamed to admit it, but through the failure I have seen the need.

MARILEE HORTON

*L*isten, Lord,
a mother's praying
low and quiet:
listen, please.
Listen to what her tears
are saying,
see her heart
upon its knees;
lift the load
from her bowed shoulders
till she sees
and understands,
You, Who hold
the worlds together,
hold her problems
in Your hands.

RUTH BELL GRAHAM

*Every year Jesus'
parents went to Jerusalem for the Feast of the
Passover. When he was twelve years old, they
went up to the Feast, according to the custom.
After the Feast was over, while his parents were
returning home, the boy Jesus stayed behind in
Jerusalem, but they were unaware of it. Thinking he was in their company, they traveled on
for a day. Then they began looking for him
among their relatives and friends. When they
did not find him, they went back to Jerusalem
to look for him. After three days they found him
in the temple courts, sitting among the teachers,
listening to them and asking them questions.
Everyone who heard him was amazed at his
understanding and his answers. When his parents saw him, they were astonished. His mother
said to him, "Son, why have you treated us like
this? Your father and I have been anxiously
searching for you."*

*"Why were you searching for me?" he asked.
"Didn't you know I had to be in my Father's
house?" But they did not understand what he
was saying to them.*

*Then he went down to Nazareth with them
and was obedient to them. But his mother treasured all these things in her heart. And Jesus
grew in wisdom and stature, and in favor with
God and men.*

LUKE 2:41-52

NIV

*A*s mothers we often spend more time worrying about our children's social standing or health habits than their characters. We sometimes take more pride in what our children can do than in what they are.

We expend more energy thinking about what they are going to do for a living when they grow up than we do about what kind of a person they are going to be when

they grow up. We make more of an effort to change their personalities, which have little moral importance, than we do to guide their characters, in which God is most interested.

BARBARA BUSH

FOR A SECOND MOM

I'm so thankful, Mom, for your willingness to step into a bereft family and to assume the role of mother for five busy children. Looking back on that stressful period, I can only imagine the trial we put you through. Each of us, from the two-year-old to the thirteen-year-old, tested you in our own unique manner. I can only imagine that our resentments and rages were a mystery to you.

Your professional background with troubled youth in some manner prepared you for your new role as a mother. But the loss of your career and the resulting "poverty"—social, intellectual, and financial—must at times have demoralized you to the point of wondering about your ability with children in general, let alone this particular confusing mix of personalities genetically so unlike your own. We children were needy and searching for love to fill a void in our souls. We had no empathy for you—no sympathy for your needs. We've now traveled together as mom and daughter for thirty-five years. You've been my mentor, friend, and confidante over many years. You are my mom in the truest sense of the word. Thanks, Mom!

DONNA HUISJEN

$\mathcal{W}$e moms need a refuge, a place of retreat and safety when we have failed. When we have lost our last shred of control and hollered at our treasured child. When we selfishly refused to help our husband because we wanted him to handle it.

God is that safe place in such moments. He has set himself apart for us so that he is always available to meet our needs, whatever they are.

What is it you need today? Forgiveness? Hope? Strength to begin again? Why not go to your refuge? Go to God.

ELISA MORGAN

*D*iapering a baby is an eternal act that looks temporary. In that moment when a parent is leaning over her baby, and their eyes lock in a steady gaze, true bonding occurs. Parent/child intimacy doesn't spring up according to scheduled fifteen-minute intervals. It happens at 2:00 a.m. when your eyes are bloodshot and feel like they're full of gravel. In those unplanned moments, heaven hushes while a parent and child are suspended in a loving eye-to-eye embrace. It didn't feel eternal when you crawled out of bed, but it was.

Discerning what is eternal isn't easy; it is often camouflaged in the simple, ordinary things of life. The temporal is brassy and demanding and loud. It stands up and screams for our attention. But we have to train our eyes to see the eternal in the unlikely events of everyday life.

ANNIE CHAPMAN

Dear Lord,

I want this little boy to know how much I love him. I want him to know how much joy he has brought to my life. . . . Help him to know how much he is wanted.

Help me to show him how much. By the sparkle of delight in my eyes when I smile at him. By how quick I am to drop a mother's chores and play with him. By the unhurried way I read him stories, even stories I've read to him a hundred times before. Especially those stories, Lord, because they will create such a vivid memory for him.

Help me to give this boy a happy childhood, filled with late nights and pillow fights and stories read by flashlight under his covers. May his mornings be filled with building forts, his noons with peanut butter sandwiches eaten in a tree house and his afternoons with baseball with the neighbor kids.

May his childhood be filled with such happy times, Lord, that when he looks back on them, twenty, thirty, forty years hence, the memories will bring a smile to his face and a reassurance to his heart that he was wanted, and that he was loved.

**ROBERT & MARY WELLS,
KEN & JUDY GIRE**

It seems but yesterday you lay
new in my arms.
Into our lives you brought
sunshine and laughter—
play—
showers, too,
and song.
Headstrong,
heartstrong,
gay,
tender beyond believing,
simple in faith,
clear-eyed,
shy,
eager for life—
you left us
rich in memories,
little wife.
And now today
I hear you say
words wise beyond your years;
I watch you play
with your small son,
tenderest of mothers.
Years slip away—
today
we are mothers
together.

RUTH BELL GRAHAM

Naomi said, "Return home, my daughters. Why would you come with me? Am I going to have any more sons, who could become your husbands? Return home, my daughters; I am too old to have another husband. Even if I thought there was still hope for me—even if I had a husband tonight and then gave birth to sons—would you wait until they grew up? Would you remain unmarried for them? No, my daughters. It is more bitter for me than for you, because the Lord's hand has gone out against me!"

At this they wept again. Then Orpah kissed her mother-in-law good-by, but Ruth clung to her.

"Look," said Naomi, "your sister-in-law is going back to her people and her gods. Go back with her."

But Ruth replied, "Don't urge me to leave you or to turn back from you. Where you go I will go, and where you stay I will stay. Your people will be my people and your God my God. Where you die I will die, and there I will be buried. May the Lord deal with me, be it ever so severely, if anything but death separates you and me." When Naomi realized that Ruth was determined to go with her, she stopped urging her.

RUTH 1:11-18

NIV

Something wondrous happens when a woman becomes a mom.

Suddenly she begins to look at all of life a bit differently. She finds herself in the middle of two generations and sees both in a whole new light. She watches her children respond to life and experiences a renewed sense of childlikeness.

She thinks about her own childhood.

She also looks at her parents, especially her mother, in a new way. She considers the ways in which she was parented and she understands. She thinks about sibling relationships—her own and those of her children.

Often these thoughts reawaken some longings she experienced in her childhood.

Through time she learns that God creates longing in our hearts in order to draw us closer to him.

CAROL KUYKENDALL

THE TREASURE

In Mama's little treasure box
    there are some tiny, lacy socks
And a beaded bracelet that's
    too small for her to wear.
There are pictures made of scribbles,
    little bibs for catching dribbles,
And a shiny bow that's tied
    around a lock of wispy hair.

There's no insurance on this treasure.
    She says that no one can measure
Just how rich a mom is she
    with memories of her family.

PAT MATUSZAK

*M*othering without being smothered means we limit what we're willing to do for our children. It is not in a child's best interest to have a mature, capable adult at his beck and call twenty-four hours a day, waiting to feed him his favorite foods, then clean up his messes, entertain him when he's bored and pacify him when he's cranky. We're mothers, not handmaidens to royalty.

ANNIE CHAPMAN

When I was a teenager, I made it a practice to read my Bible every night before going to sleep. One night I was so weary. As I sat on the side of my bed castigating myself for being lazy, my mom came to my room for a brief bedtime visit.

"What are you doing?" she asked.

"Just sitting here thinking I should read my Bible and pray, but I really don't feel like it."

"Honey," she said as she came to sit on the bed beside me, "God is not a hard taskmaster. He understands our weakness. Just go to sleep."

My mother probably never knew what freedom she gave me in that moment. She helped me understand that God knows all about his children and that sometimes the most spiritual thing we can do is just to rest. I have never forgotten her words, and I have thought of them again and again when I'm tempted to beat myself up for being human with human frailties. Thanks, Mom!

GWEN ELLIS

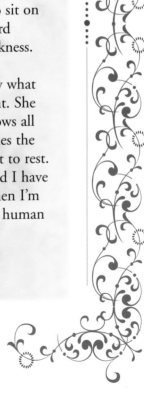

*L*ord, didn't I wash these same
dishes yesterday?
Make the same beds?
Scrub the same floor?
Rout the same dust?
Launder the same clothes?
How can I ever catch up?
Even when I prepare a great meal,
we need feeding again a short while later.

Nothing stays done, Lord!
Nothing ever stays neat
or clean
or finished . . .
And no one ever stays fed!
No wonder housewifery
has such a bad name!

But, Lord,
you do the same thing every
day,
Bringing the sun up,
placing the clouds,
darkening the sky at evening . . .
yet your work is done with such a flair
as to delight the heart!
My tasks are humble, Lord,
but necessary.

> **All that I am or ever hope to be, I owe to my angel Mother.**
>
> **ABRAHAM LINCOLN**

Let me do them graciously
with loving-kindness and good humor.
And please, Lord,
teach me to deal creatively
with dishes
and dust curls!

MARGARET B. SPIESS

*esus went to a town
called Nain, and his
disciples and a large crowd went along with
him. As he approached the town gate, a dead
person was being carried out—the only son of
his mother, and she was a widow. And a large
crowd from the town was with her. When the
Lord saw her, his heart went out to her and he
said, "Don't cry."*

*Then he went up and touched the coffin,
and those carrying it stood still. He said,
"Young man, I say to you, get up!" The dead
man sat up and began to talk, and Jesus gave
him back to his mother.*

*They were all filled with awe and praised
God.*

LUKE 7:11-16

One day in the mountain region of Scotland, a gigantic eagle snatched a little baby out of his crib and flew away with him. The people of the village ran out after the big bird, but the eagle perched itself upon a nearby mountain crag. Could the child possibly be rescued? A sailor tried to climb the ascent, but he was at last obliged to give up the attempt. A robust Highlander, accustomed to climbing those mountains, tried next and even his strength failed. At last a poor peasant woman came forward. She put her feet upon one shelf on the rock, then on the second, then on the third and in this manner she rose to the very top of the cliff. While all below held their breath for sheer fright, she came down step by step until she stood at the bottom of the rock with the child safely in her arms. Immediately shouts of praise arose from the crowd that had gathered.

Why did that woman succeed when the strong sailor and the experienced mountain climber had failed? Because that woman was the mother of the baby. Her love for her baby had given her the courage to do what the others had failed to do.

HENRIETTA MEARS

Mother's Love

Her love is like an island in Life's
ocean, vast and wide,
    A peaceful, quiet
shelter from the
wind, and rain,
and tide.

    'Tis bound on
the north by Hope,
by Patience on
the west,
    By tender
Counsel on the
south, and on the
east by Rest.

    Above it like a
beacon light shine
Faith, and Truth,
and Prayer;
    And through the changing scenes of life,
I find a haven there.

AUTHOR UNKNOWN

A wife of noble
character who can find?
She is worth far more than rubies.
Her husband has full
    confidence in her
    and lacks nothing of
    value.
She brings him good, not
    harm, all the days of
    her life.
She selects wool and flax
    and works with eager
    hands.
She is like the merchant ships,
    bringing her food from
    afar.
She gets up while it is still
    dark; she provides food for
    her family and portions
    for her servant girls.
She considers a field and buys
    it; out of her earnings she plants a vineyard.
She sets about her work vigorously;
    her arms are strong for her tasks.
She sees that her trading is profitable,
    and her lamp does not go out at night.
In her hand she holds the distaff
    and grasps the spindle with her fingers.
She opens her arms to the poor
    and extends her hands to the needy.

When it snows, she has no fear for her
    household;
        for all of them are clothed in scarlet.
She makes coverings for her bed;
        she is clothed in fine linen and purple.
Her husband is respected at the city gate,
        where he takes his seat among the elders
        of the land.
She makes linen garments and sells them,
        and supplies the merchants with sashes.
She is clothed with strength and dignity;
        she can laugh at the days to come.
She speaks with wisdom,
        and faithful instruction is on her tongue.
She watches over the affairs of her household
        and does not eat the bread of idleness.
Her children arise and call her blessed;
        her husband also, and he praises her:
"Many women do noble things,
        but you surpass them all."
Charm is deceptive, and beauty is fleeting;
        but a woman who fears the Lord is to
        be praised.
Give her the reward she has earned,
        and let her works bring her praise at
        the city gate.

PROVERBS 31:10-31

NIV

Like growing a garden, raising children is a difficult kind of joy. Mothers generally come to the task without prior training or household help. Maybe we rocked our baby brother or babysat, but Mom did the rest. For most of us, launching into twenty-four-hour-a-day care is a consuming task.

We can easily lose sight of the good growth taking hold in our children by focusing on the negatives, much like struggling over one little weed in our garden and failing to see the rows of gorgeous flowers. If you are doing your best, you may need to lay down your tools, sit back and look down that row. We only work the field. God grows the plants.

NANCY CORBETT COLE

Where does it stop? There seems to be no end to the demands and expectations placed on women today. We are all plagued by time pressure. I am sure all of us have felt, at one time or another, that everything is coming in on us, that we are never finished, never caught up. The queen in Alice in Wonderland said, "It takes all the running you can do to stay in place. If you want to get someplace else, you must run twice as fast as that." How true this seems today. I sometimes find myself running, and if I take a moment to ask why, I can't find a good reason.

Being too busy has become a compulsion for many and a way of life for most. . . . The effects of being too busy are beginning to take their toll. . . . I have a hard time believing this kind of busyness is pleasing to the Lord.

GIGI GRAHAM TCHIVIDJIAN

I doubt, Mom, that you knew when you got dressed that morning how much your shoes would mean to me. Well, not your shoes really, but your footsteps. That was in days when suburban women donned dresses and high heels to take the bus downtown rather than jumping into jeans and Nikes and taking the Grand Cherokee.

I was nine and was confined to complete bed rest for three days in the hospital. Every afternoon when you came to visit, I could hear the sound of your high-heeled shoes on the linoleum floor in the corridor. I heard them as you made your way down the long hall from the elevator and knew you were coming to be with me.

> **God isn't completely free to work in a child's life until we let go of that child and leave him or her entirely in God's hands.**
>
> **MARGIE M. LEWIS**

So many women, when they walk in high heels, sound businesslike, bustling, impatient. Yours were more measured, quiet, dignified. When I heard your familiar footsteps outside the ward, it meant the end of long hours of being scared, bored, and lonely. I have had three babies and faced several surgeries for breast cancer. And whenever you visit me in the hospital, it's still the same. Your footsteps have come to mean to me, "Mom is coming. Everything will be fine."

RUTH DEJAGER

When my children were very young, some days I felt they would never grow up. At the end of a wearying day of changing a dozen diapers, attending to unhappy cries, and engaging in baby talk, I was convinced my brain was slowly and irrevocably atrophying. I wasn't merely losing a few brain cells, mind you; I was teetering on the brink of mental retardation. I wondered wistfully if I would ever again be able to go into the bathroom without a baby crawling after me, or leave the house without slinging Kristen on one hip, trailing little Holly by the hand, and wrestling with a bulging diaper bag.

Knowing little about the developmental stages of a woman's life, it never occurred to me to reflect on the panoramic sweep of a woman's existence, start to finish. Had I done so, I might have realized the years of child rearing were only one rich, valuable portion of my life span—a season to be cherished and enjoyed.

BRENDA HUNTER

When I was younger, I thought my mom didn't know anything. After all, she grew up in another era! Everything is different now! But as time went by, I learned that she does know some things.

Mom told me the basic things every mother says such as, "Make sure you eat enough vegetables," and "You need eight hours of sleep." But more than that, she taught me about the way I should live. She taught me about relationships.

"If you chase men," she said, "they will run." She also advised me, "If you love someone, sometimes you do things for him even if you don't want to." The qualities she has instilled in me—such as compassion and faith in God—and the inheritance she has passed on to me—such as joy and wisdom— are not only qualities I strive for in myself, but are also those I look for in friends.

The two pieces of advice I consider most valuable are these: "Just because you love someone doesn't mean he is the right person for you." And, "Be with people who make you want to be a better person. It is important that the people around you encourage your virtues and not your vices."

As each year passes I understand more and more that my mom is not telling me what to do, but rather is sharing with me those bits of learning, experience, and wisdom that make her the blessed person she is today.

JULIE BLAUWKAMP

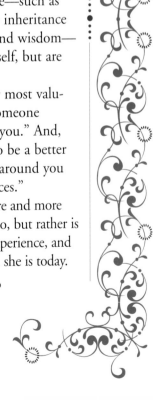

ost mothers I've talked to admit they "get buggy" if they don't do something creative during the day. Wanting to do something besides talk in toddler sentences is not frivolous; we need not feel guilty for being created that way! "In the image of God" we were created, and certainly God is the master of creativity and imagination.

MELODIE M. DAVIS

After he was weaned, [Hannah] took the boy with her…and brought him to the house of the Lord at Shiloh. When they had slaughtered the bull, they brought the boy to Eli, and she said to him, "As surely as you live, my lord, I am the woman who stood here beside you praying to the LORD. I prayed for this child, and the LORD has granted me what I asked of him. So now I give him to the LORD. For his whole life he will be given over to the LORD." And he worshiped the LORD there.

Then Hannah prayed and said:
"My heart rejoices in the LORD;
in the LORD my horn is lifted high.
My mouth boasts over my enemies,
for I delight in your deliverance.

"There is no one holy like the LORD;
there is no one besides you;
there is no Rock like our God.

"Do not keep talking so proudly
or let your mouth speak such arrogance,
for the LORD is a God who knows,
and by him deeds are weighed.

"The bows of the warriors are broken,
but those who stumbled are armed with strength.

"Those who were full hire themselves out for food,
but those who were hungry hunger no more.
She who was barren has borne seven children,
but she who has had many sons pines away.

"The LORD brings death and makes alive;
he brings down to the grave and raises up.
The LORD sends poverty and wealth;
he humbles and he exalts.
He raises the poor from the dust
and lifts the needy from the ash heap;
he seats them with princes
and has them inherit a throne of honor.

"For the foundations of the earth are the LORD's;
upon them he has set the world.
He will guard the feet of his saints,
but the wicked will be silenced in darkness.

"It is not by strength that one prevails;
those who oppose the LORD will be shattered.
He will thunder against them from heaven;
the LORD will judge the ends of the earth.

"He will give strength to his king
and exalt the horn of his anointed."

Then Elkanah [and Hannah] went home to
Ramah, but the boy ministered before the LORD
under Eli the priest.

1 SAMUEL 1:24-2:11

NIV

A while back I saw a bumper sticker that read, "Life is short. Eat dessert first." Though pigging out on dessert isn't wise dieting advice, I liked the slogan. To me it said, "Lighten up." Homes will not break up, children will not go to bed hungry, and the sun will not fall from the sky if I miss double-coupon day or fail to get my thighs in shape. We've got to keep touch with reality. God wants us to be obedient, not obsessive. Living simply means concentrating on what's important in light of eternity, and not taking the rest of life too seriously.

ANNIE CHAPMAN

I challenge you, I admonish you, I encourage you to recognize that the children God has given you are sinners who must be pointed to the Savior. Make it your goal to return your children to the King as saints who are well-prepared to live their lives for Jesus. Don't make the priority returning to Him beauty queens, brilliant scholars, successful career persons, or wealthy entrepreneurs. Lead them first to be lovers of Jesus.

DONNA OTTO

*O*ne mother, whose two children are almost grown, summarized what mother after mother told me when she said, "The most helpful thing I ever found for dealing with my stress as a mother was my friendships with other mothers. I wish as a young mother I had taken more time to develop friendships. I don't know why I didn't. Maybe I was just too wrapped up in the newness and the stress of young children. But I didn't learn until later how important such friendships are."

DEBORAH SHAW LEWIS

*N*ow two prostitutes came to [Solomon] and stood before him. One of them said, "My lord, this woman and I live in the same house. I had a baby while she was there with me. The third day after my child was born, this woman also had a baby. We were alone; there was no one in the house but the two of us.

"During the night this woman's son died because she lay on him. So she got up in the middle of the night and took my son from my side while I your servant was asleep. She put him by her breast and put her dead son by my breast. The next morning, I got up to nurse my son—and he was dead! But when I looked at him closely in the morning light, I saw that it wasn't the son I had borne."

The other woman said, "No! The living one is my son; the dead one is yours."

But the first one insisted, "No! The dead one is yours; the living one is mine." And so they argued before the king.

The king said, "This one says, 'My son is alive and your son is dead,' while that one says, 'No! Your son is dead and mine is alive.'"

Then the king said, "Bring me a sword." So they brought a sword for the king. He then gave an order: "Cut the living child in two and give half to one and half to the other."

The woman whose son was alive was filled with compassion for her son and said to the king, "Please, my lord, give her the living baby! Don't kill him!"

But the other said, "Neither I nor you shall have him. Cut him in two!"

Then the king gave his ruling: "Give the living baby to the first woman. Do not kill him; she is his mother."

1 KINGS 3:16-27
NIV

Impatience is the root of most tensions in both home and workplace. More arguments begin in the home through impatience than anything else. Thinking, "I've had it," and letting words fly is never the best action, no matter how justified you may believe you are.

The next time you're tempted to fly off the handle and say things you'll regret, or give up on something before you've seen fulfillment, remember Noah and his wife and their patience. They endured and saw God's promise become reality.

NANCY CORBETT COLE

*I*t is crucial to focus on the relationship our work has to God's work. If we are meeting legitimate needs, our work is God's work. We are partners with him in the ongoing care and development of his universe. He asks us to do our best, but never alone. We are standing beside Jesus, joining him in the joy of participating in work he created us to do.

What does this mean? He is present when you need help. He is as adept in your laundry room or boardroom as at church. Because it is his work, he is a remarkable source of wisdom for any difficult problem you might face. All you have to do is ask. Because you are his design, he is your best source of guidance as you choose your tasks.

KATHY PEEL

> *Oh, cleaning and scrubbing will wait till tomorrow, but children grow up, as I've learned to my sorrow. So quiet down cobwebs. Dust go to sleep. I'm rocking my baby. Babies don't keep.*
>
> **RUTH HULBURT HAMILTON**

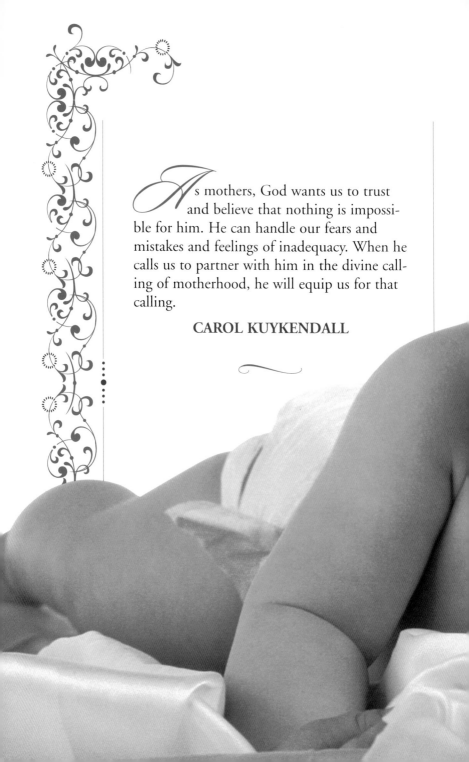

As mothers, God wants us to trust and believe that nothing is impossible for him. He can handle our fears and mistakes and feelings of inadequacy. When he calls us to partner with him in the divine calling of motherhood, he will equip us for that calling.

CAROL KUYKENDALL

I have forgiven death for too soon taking from me my child, whom I needed so much. I have forgiven life for the supreme hurt. Death has become acceptable. But sorrow never leaves one at the same place she is found. What has emerged is a new me, reaching out for the riches of nonmaterialistic values, stronger, softer, and more understanding.

I look down and lovingly touch the gold and diamond *#1* on a delicate chain around my neck, a Christmas gift from my husband and son. Closing my eyes, I hear Kim's voice once more, "Mom, good ol' mom. Next to God, you're number one."

BETH JAMESON

*B*eing a good mom isn't complicated. Only one thing is needed. When we, ourselves, dine on the presence of Jesus, our children will find in us what they need.

ELISA MORGAN

As a mother, I was obligated to meet my daughter's needs. But what a joy it was when I could delight her heart by giving her some of the fun stuff, too—surprises, a few things I knew she wanted, extras — just for the pure pleasure.

Our Father's giving is like that— only much, much more! He is the perfect parent . . . , and he wants to supply

both our needs and our wants—what we need for health and what is for pure joy. God does indeed delight to delight in each of us.

CAROLE MAYHALL

For some reason, we mothers tend to think that the more we do for our family the better we are at our job, and we feel guilty when we begin to cut the apron strings. But the general attitude among our moms is that you do your child a big favor when you teach him to take on responsibility as soon as he is able.

I heard songwriter and author Gloria Gaither say once that a mother's primary goal should be to work herself out of a job. That's hard to accept, because it means gradually making yourself physically, although not emotionally, dispensable to your child. But it's the only way to raise capable, responsible, emotionally healthy children.

KAREN HULL

Had I been Joseph's mother
I'd have prayed
protection from his brothers:
"God keep him safe;
he is so young
so different from
the others."
Mercifully
she never knew
there would be slavery
and prison, too.

Had I been Moses' mother
I'd have wept
to keep my little son;
praying she might forget
the babe drawn from the water
of the Nile,
had I not kept
him for her
nursing him the while?
Was he not mine
and she
but Pharaoh's daughter?

Had I been Daniel's mother
I should have pled
"Give victory!

This Babylonian horde—
godless and cruel—
don't let them take him captive
—better dead,
Almighty Lord!"

Had I been Mary—
Oh, had I been she,
I would have cried
as never mother cried,
". . . Anything, O God,
anything . . .
but crucified!"

With such prayers
importunate
my finite wisdom
would assail
Infinite Wisdom;

God how fortunate
Infinite Wisdom
should prevail!

RUTH BELL GRAHAM

We cannot go with our children into adulthood; they will have to conquer their own ground, as we did. But we can keep the home fires burning and the welcome mat out, sensitive to the signals we receive from their battleground and ready for a time when our young adult needs a temporary "R and R" or a chance to fall back and regroup. "Having done everything," we can only cover them in the armor of our prayers as they go forward.

CAROLYN JOHNSON

Ask the primary question: "What does my child need?" The answer is not necessarily clean pillowcases, vegetables, and proper bedtimes. The answer is: Our children need us to be the guardians of the trust, the protectors of family relationships, parents with clear focus and pure hearts. They need us to have faithful hearts—to care deeply, passionately, and affectionately for them.

VALERIE BELL

The mother makes up her mind to a certain course of action, which she believes to be right and best. The children clamor against it and declare it shall not be. But the mother, knowing that she is mistress and not they, pursues her course lovingly and calmly in spite of all their clamors; and the result is that the children are sooner or later won over to the mother's course of action, and fall in with her decision, and all is harmonious and happy.

HANNAH WHITALL SMITH

In tenderness He sought me,
Weary and sick with sin,
And on His shoulders brought me
Back to His fold again;
While angels in His presence sang
Until the courts of heaven rang.
Oh, the love that sought me!
Oh, the blood that bought me!
Oh, the grace that brought me to the fold,
Wondrous grace that brought me to the
fold!

This hymn by W. Spencer Walton goes back to the early days of my childhood in China, and I have loved it ever since. If in tenderness He sought me, will He not in equal tenderness seek mine?

RUTH BELL GRAHAM

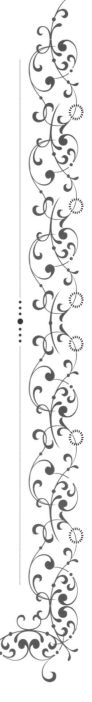

The single most important decision a mother can make is to develop her own life with God. Unless she nurtures herself spiritually first, she will have no base from which to have a positive spiritual influence on her children.

Scripture reveals God's agenda for making a spiritual impact on our children: We must begin with ourselves; then we must teach our children.

In Deuteronomy 6:6-7, God first tells parents, "These commandments that I give you today are to be upon your hearts." Then he says, "Impress them on your children."

JEAN FLEMING

*M*y mother and I are very different from each other. I've probably never quite been the daughter she expected. As a child, I didn't play with dolls very much; I preferred playing ball with my brothers. I often had my nose buried in a book. I don't sew, bake, or cook. Rather than staying home to take care of my husband and children, I became a career woman. Mom, on the other hand, is a homebody. She made our lunches, baked cookies, and made soup. Her full-time job was taking care of her husband and kids.

In spite of our differences in lifestyle, I have always felt my mother's love and support for doing what I felt called to and gifted for. Mom's love became very practical when my children were still small and were sick. She volunteered to stay with them. Even now, when she comes for dinner, she brings cookies and dessert. Best of all, she still affirms me and freely expresses her love and pride. I love my mother for who she is and what she does for our family, but I especially love her for letting me be who I am.

CAROLINE BLAUWKAMP

When I picture a mother wisely using all of life to impress God's truth on the lives of her children, I am profoundly challenged. I want to do all I can to make my home a "learning tree."

Such effective, timely teaching must be an overflow of our lives. We can't share with our children what we don't know ourselves. The right words won't automatically roll from our lips. Our readiness depends on our intake of the Bible and our fellowship with God.

JEAN FLEMING

*T*here it was, right in front of me. With six children, it was obvious that my season, for now, was home, homemaking, mothering; that it was there that I would bring forth my fruit; there is where I would prosper.

I know that since my "season" is homemaking, the care of my family is to top my priority list. Right now, that occupies most of my time, but circumstances change, children grow up, responsibilities shift. With the children now in school most of the day, I have found I have a little more time for something else. This is where I have to consider carefully, before Him, any new field of interest or activity; I have to expand prudently and be careful not to neglect my present God-given responsibilities.

GIGI GRAHAM TCHIVIDJIAN

The mother's heart is the child's schoolroom.

HENRY WARD BEECHER

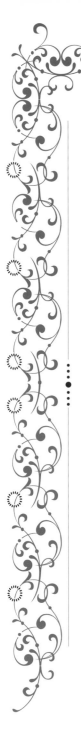

The highest function of my motherly love would be fulfilled when my love was strong enough to cut the apron strings and let my adult child move off into his own life. I would succeed as a mother only when I had so reared my child that he would no longer have need of me. Yet this is not tragedy; it is growth. This is no betrayal of love. This is love.

CATHERINE MARSHALL

Who ran to help me when I fell,
And would some pretty story tell,
Or kiss the place to make it well?
My mother.

JANE TAYLOR

Children are the anchors that hold a mother to life.

SOPHOCLES

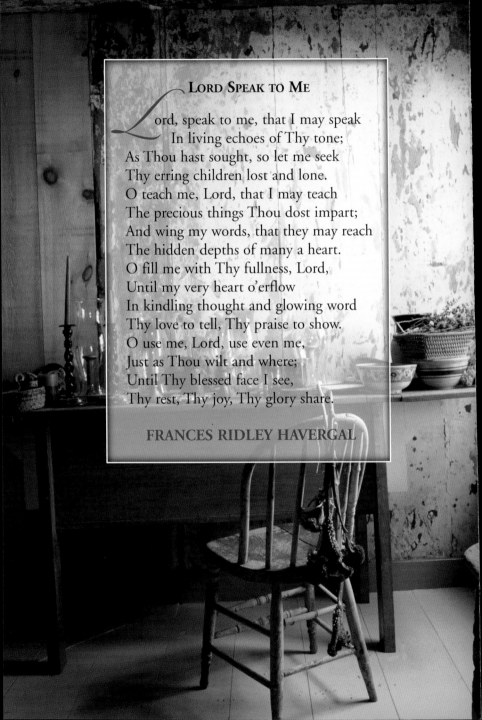

LORD SPEAK TO ME

Lord, speak to me, that I may speak
    In living echoes of Thy tone;
As Thou hast sought, so let me seek
Thy erring children lost and lone.
O teach me, Lord, that I may teach
The precious things Thou dost impart;
And wing my words, that they may reach
The hidden depths of many a heart.
O fill me with Thy fullness, Lord,
Until my very heart o'erflow
In kindling thought and glowing word
Thy love to tell, Thy praise to show.
O use me, Lord, use even me,
Just as Thou wilt and where;
Until Thy blessed face I see,
Thy rest, Thy joy, Thy glory share.

FRANCES RIDLEY HAVERGAL

I like being a mother, and I can't give up without some regret an era of my life that I've enjoyed. The passing of this era not only makes me nostalgic but also makes me face the reality of my own physical mortality. Just as the death of both my parents gave me a raw, unsettling awareness of a generation gone by, so the emptying of our nest will edge me a step closer to my own passing.

CAROL KUYKENDALL

*T*he lonely hours
Have become for me
Very precious hours indeed.
Because
In reality
I found that I was not
alone.
Jesus gently
Reminded me
That
I was His own.

GIGI GRAHAM TCHIVIDJIAN

*W*hat a lioness
was your mother among the lions!
She lay down among the young lions
and reared her cubs.

Your mother was like a vine in your vineyard
planted by the water;
it was fruitful and full of branches
because of abundant water.

EZEKIEL 19:2,10

NIV

*W*e mothers need time each week to develop gifts. If we paint, we need to find a few hours to set up the easels and uncap the watercolors. If our passion is for gardening, let us plant, hoe, and prune whenever we can. A garden can be a work of art.

So make home the studio where we unfurl our canvases, unsheathe our garden shears, up our word processors . . . and lose ourselves a few hours each week in creativity. We will, if we do it with diligence, be surprised where our gifts take us—and how they restore our emotional energy.

BRENDA HUNTER

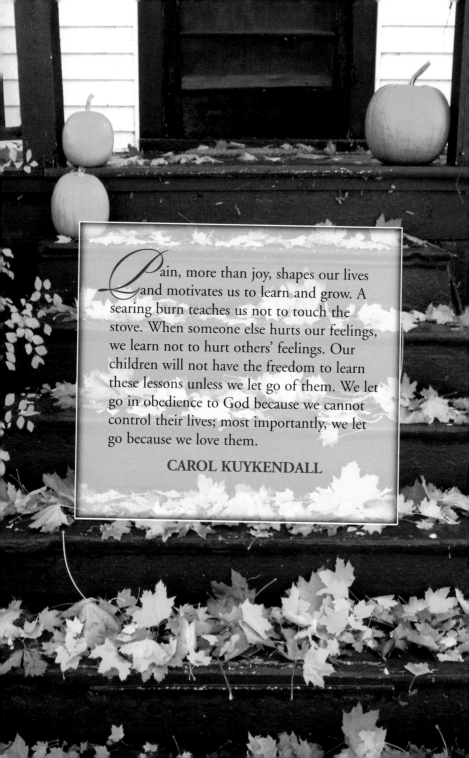

Pain, more than joy, shapes our lives and motivates us to learn and grow. A searing burn teaches us not to touch the stove. When someone else hurts our feelings, we learn not to hurt others' feelings. Our children will not have the freedom to learn these lessons unless we let go of them. We let go in obedience to God because we cannot control their lives; most importantly, we let go because we love them.

CAROL KUYKENDALL

What is taking place within your womb is a miracle, but it happens so slowly we take it for granted. After all, nine months is a long time to wait for a miracle.

During those nine months God is not only preparing a baby for the parents, he is preparing the parents for the baby. So much has to be rearranged to accommodate this new life—not just making room in your home but making room in your heart.

And that takes time.

God could have performed the miracle in "quick motions," and it would have turned everybody's head; but he chose to do it slowly, content to turn only yours.

Of course, some of the brimming wonder will spill over to your husband, just as Mary's wonder spilled over to Joseph. But it was she who felt the flutter of the Christ-child within, she who nourished the fragile life, she who pondered the miracle in her heart. To Joseph it was given only to feel the child's movements from the outside, only to nourish the child's mother, only to be midwife to the miracle.

For nine months your husband will know this child only from afar, but you will know it from deep within you. For within you it will live and move and grow. What you eat, it will eat. Where you go, it will go. For nine months you will be one with this miracle.

ROBERT & MARY WELLS
KEN & JUDY GIRE

I recently watched a sitcom in which a grown daughter lamented the fact that her mother hadn't been there for her as a child. All she really wanted, she cried, was a mother who would bake her cookies, read her books, and put Band-Aids on her hurts.

This TV character's words made me realize how much those little things meant to me as a child. Some of my fondest memories are of picking flowers in the woods, creating my own little masterpieces at kitchen table craft sessions and long talks in the car on the way to the store--all times spent with my own mother. Of course, Mom made many large sacrifices for me through the years for which I will always be grateful. But it is those little things that define what "Mom" means to me and that cause me to think of my own mom with a full heart and a smile.

MOLLY DETWEILER

*W*e cannot do great things. We can only do little things with great love.

MOTHER TERESA

I'm concerned for the working mom. I'm one. As most working moms realize, professional demands must coexist with family concerns . . . . More and more Christian women are hoping to "dance well" and someday win the Proverbs 31 mother's double blessing of praise from her family and praise for her work at the city gate. We, who are mothers, must be careful, though, that our society's preference for praise-giving at the city gates does not seduce us from our priority work, that less praised work of nurturing our families.

VALERIE BELL

*E*ver since I was young, I have watched my mother's example, and I have learned much about waiting and building. Her life has been one of much waiting and much giving. She built a place of shelter—her ark—virtually alone, with daddy away so much of the time. The waiting periods were often long and quite difficult . . . .

When she had nothing left to give, she went to the source of her strength and the supplier of all her needs and was unexplainably replenished. So much so, that we children never saw or knew of her needs. She gave us the sunshine, and gave Jesus all the rest.

GIGI GRAHAM TCHIVIDJIAN

There was never a child so lovely but his mother was glad to get him asleep.

RALPH WALDO EMERSON

*S*usanna Wesley, Corrie ten Boom, Catherine Booth, Florence Nightingale. These women changed the world. Their stories moved me to want to do the same. But they also gave me another gift: they showed me the secrets of how such influence grows. From them I learned that the ripple effect happens over the course of a lifetime. And the real magnitude of our impact may not be felt until after we've died. Faithfully serving wherever God planted them was the key to these women's lives. We serve with joy wherever He chooses, and He causes the ripples from our service to spread to the world.

ANNIE CHAPMAN

Like other shepherds
help me keep
watch o'er my flock by night;
mindful of each need,
each hurt, which might
lead one to stray—
each weakness
and each ill—
while others sleep
teach me to pray.
At night the wolves and leopards,
hungry and clever, prowl
in search of strays
and wounded; when they howl,
Lord, still my anxious heart
to calm delight—
for the Great Shepherd
watches with me
over my flock
by night.

RUTH BELL GRAHAM

aring for children is one of life's most demanding roles. Nurturing children requires the delicacy of a diamond-cutter, the strength of a sculptress, the tenacity of a weaver, and the undying vision of a painter. It's not easy. The raw materials—children—are by nature hard to handle, uncooperative, willful. But there's nothing more valuable or beautiful to behold than a well-reared child. Diamonds pale and fortunes fade when compared to a child who's on his way to making a positive contribution to humanity.

VALERIE BELL

There's a way in which mothering is instinctive. A mom intrinsically knows her child. The library of maternal instinct teaches moms to trust this instinctive response. Few of us have to be taught to cuddle a baby who is upset. Most of us respond immediately to her cry and can quickly interpret its meaning. Sometimes we wake in the night before he even starts to whimper. Having taken no courses on cooing, babbling, or giggling with our infants, we naturally respond when they speak in this "language."

ELISA MORGAN
CAROL KUYKENDALL

I searched—
but there definitely was not
a packet of instructions
attached to my children
when they arrived.
    And none has since
        landed in my mailbox.
            Lord, show me how
        to be a good parent.
            Teach me to
        correct without crushing,
        help without hanging on,
        listen without laughing,
        surround without
        smothering,
and love without limit—
The way You love me.

SUSAN L. LENZKES

> *Of all the rights of women, the greatest is to be a mother.*
>
> **LIN YUTANG**

All her instinct as a woman—the eternal nourisher of children, of men, of society—demands that she give. Her time, her energy, her creativeness drain out into these channels if there is any chance, any leak. Traditionally we are taught, and instinctively we long, to give where it is needed—and immediately. Eternally, woman spills herself away in driblets to the thirsty, seldom being allowed the time, the quiet, the peace to let the pitcher fill up to the brim.

ANNE MORROW LINDBERGH

The mother who can laugh at herself, with her children, and at the impossible situations of life, is far ahead on the road to personal control.

GRACE KETTERMAN
PAT HOLT

Since my children, like yours, have grown up in a very different world from that of my childhood, with a barrage of competing messages and values, I wanted to share with them in this book what I was taught to remember and what I have learned from reading, meditation, prayer, silence, personal experience and struggle as I have tried to discern and carry out the tasks assigned to me. I want my children to know the values I hold most dear, which do not change no matter the times; that they are in my thoughts and prayers often every day; and that each occupies a very special room in my heart and owns love that is his alone and that can never be occupied by another or taken away by anything he can ever say or do.

MARIAN WRIGHT EDELMAN

By and large, mothers and housewives are the only workers who do not have regular time off. They are the great vacationless class.

ANNE MORROW LINDBERGH

aith shines brightest in the heart
of a child.

H.G. BOSCH

$\mathcal{P}$erspective is the ability to stand between yesterday and tomorrow and understand how and where today fits in. As the mothers of young children seeking to discover how our "todays" fit into our lifetime roles as women, we have to stand back and get a larger view of the whole of life. We have to identify some goals that transcend today and then remember what we're aiming toward.

Perspective means looking beyond the moment with a view toward the whole of life. And moms of preschoolers need perspective as they move through days in which the goal of a clean house can take precedence over tickle-wars, and completing a to-do list may win out over laptime.

**ELISA MORGAN
CAROL KUYKENDALL**

*I*f I could stand aside and see
  him walking through
    Those Splendor'd Gates thrown wide,
instead of me—
If I could yield my place
to this, my boy,
the tears upon my upturned face
would be of joy!

RUTH BELL GRAHAM

ow much of mothering we miss because our focus is simply on making it through! Sure, we all seethe in the face of well-intentioned advice from kindly grandmothers in grocery stores who tell us (as we wrestle with three cranky kids in the check-out line), "These are the best days of your life! Enjoy them because they pass so quickly!"

"Not quickly enough," we mutter under our breath.

But these women do have a point. One that comes with the wisdom of their years. The stage of mothering young children is a stage. It only feels like an era! And it will pass. It will not last forever. It will end one day.

When we accept the myth that the best we can do is to simply "grin and bear it," we miss out on what mothering can mean. While we're wishing ourselves into the next season, we miss the good stuff that's happening now.

**ELISA MORGAN
CAROL KUYKENDALL**

I've often wondered why children don't come with a warning label. When we brought our first child home from the hospital, I didn't know I had committed myself for the next twelve months to functioning in a state somewhere between comatose and catatonic. Neither did I realize that I'd signed over my rights to carry on an uninterrupted adult conversation for the next eighteen months.

KATHY PEEL

A hundred years from now it will not matter what my bank account was, the sort of house I lived in, or the kind of car I drove . . . but the world may be different because I was important in the life of a child.

ANONYMOUS

This week you have the opportunity to get on the floor and build block towers. This is the season when you are invited to read, to play, to imagine, to dream! Your lap is the "favorite-est place to be." Your smile is more valuable than money. Your words mean more than those on the television, in a magazine, or in a classroom. Savor the moments of this season that will never come around again.

We tend to believe that life will get better when, really, it just gets different. If the grass looks greener on the other side of your fence, it may be because you're not investing your time and energy in your own grass. Live in the present.

**ELISA MORGAN
CAROL KUYKENDALL**

Oh, time! Be slow!
  it was a dawn ago
  I was a child
dreaming of being grown;
a noon ago
  I was
with children of my own;
and now
it's afternoon
—and late—
and they are grown
and gone.
Time, wait!

RUTH BELL GRAHAM

Although I entered motherhood rather flippantly, through the years I've come to see my role not only as a big responsibility, but also a great privilege. I've found that the greatest child-raising philosopher and mentor of all time is my Heavenly Father. As he lovingly deals with me as his child, he teaches me how to parent my children.

KATHY PEEL

I know that what we write on the heart of a child cannot be erased, and when a mother is at home to contribute to the indelible marks that are written on a child's tender heart, it is a rich heritage.

BARBARA JOHNSON

Yesterday I found a fingernail
    in the toaster,
        Today the dryer yields just seven socks.
Ah, mysteries of life:
Whence fingernails?
Where socks?

          Where are the mates?
          And why not six or eight?

          I long to search for Holy Grails
          Or even joust at windmills . . .
          Instead, I rewash glasses
          Left less than spot-free
          By eager childish hands
          And hang sheets out on
              windy days
          And never do catch sight
Of one brave armored knight.

But when a little boy thanks God at night
For "the best mommy in the world"—
Strange windmills lose their charm
And I'm content
To fetch a grail of water
Before he goes to sleep.
Quixote, wait another year!
I still am needed here.

JOY JACOBS

Love the LORD your God with all your heart and with all your soul and with all your strength. These commandments that I give you today are to be upon your hearts. Impress them on your children. Talk about them when you sit at home and when you walk along the road, when you lie down and when you get up. Tie them as symbols on your hands and bind them on your foreheads. Write them on the doorframes of your houses and on your gates.

DEUTERONOMY 6:5-9

NIV

I try, Lord,
    I really do try to be a good mother!
("Maybe I try too hard?")
I must learn to give help
only when asked,
and not assume
I always know what's needed.
Things change so fast
I need a barometer to gauge moods
or a scorecard
to identify the players and their positions!
Let me be perceptive.
I want to uphold,
not nag, my children.

I'm often inflexible
when I need to be adaptable, Lord.
I must allow them
to make their own mistakes
and learn from them.
My trouble is
I love not wisely
but too well.

I wonder
now and then
why I ever applied for the job!
(Yes, I wouldn't have it otherwise.)

Guard my relationship
with each of my children, Lord.
Sometimes it's a fragile, tenuous thing.
Give them patience with me.
When I'm tired
or angry
or hurt,
control my tone of voice,
my words
and even the furrows in my brow, Lord,
so they can detect
beyond and underneath the scolding
the true love I bear them.

And help me, Lord,
to hold those I love
in an open hand.

MARGARET B. SPIESS

I remember my mother's prayers
and they have always followed me.
They have clung to me all my life.

ABRAHAM LINCOLN

My mother was the most beautiful woman I ever saw. All I am I owe to my mother. I attribute all my success in life to the moral, intellectual and physical education I received from her.

GEORGE WASHINGTON

*N*ear the cross of Jesus
stood his mother, his mother's sister, Mary the
wife of Clopas, and Mary Magdalene. When
Jesus saw his mother there, and the disciple
whom he loved standing nearby, he said to his
mother, "Dear woman, here is your son," and to
the disciple, "Here is your mother." From that
time on, this disciple took her into his home.

JOHN 19:25-27

NIV

*W*e continually
remember before our God and Father your
work produced by faith, your labor prompted
by love, and your endurance inspired by hope
in our Lord Jesus Christ.

I THESSALONIANS 1:3

Do not be anxious about anything, but in everything, by prayer and petition, with thanksgiving, present your requests to God. And the peace of God, which transcends all understanding, will guard your hearts and your minds in Christ Jesus.

PHILIPPIANS 4:6-7

Let the beloved of the LORD rest secure in him, for he shields him all day long.

DEUTERONOMY 33:12

Youth fades; love droops; the leaves of friendship fall; A mother's secret hope outlives them all.

OLIVER WENDELL HOLMES

*T*oday I went to see a movie. I needed the escape, and escape I did. Before my eyes—in two short hours—boys became men, and men became heroes. One hundred years before my time, men were dying for things I take completely for granted. I learned of their courage, their dreams, their valor. I watched as great things were achieved. I came to understand that great prices were paid.

And then, my great things to do—milk, bread, chicken, orange juice, graham crackers: grocery day.

I always wanted to change the world. But choosing peanut butter? ("Choosy mothers choose…") Without this child, would I have done great things? Am I really doing something great selecting the softest tissues?

The truth is, I would bravely go to the ends of the earth for my son. But thus far I have not been asked to. Instead, I am asked to go bravely around the block a million times. How hard it is to be a hero in the ordinary life.

ROBIN RICE MORRIS

I think it harder,
   Lord, to cast
the cares of those I love
on You,
than to cast mine.
We, growing older,
learn at last
that You
are merciful
and kind.
Not one time
have You failed me,
Lord—
why fear that you'll
fail mine?

RUTH BELL GRAHAM

I have now progressed to the point that if I don't put cookies and milk out, I know I'm not a failure as a mother. I have taken myself out of the box I built, labeled "Good Mother," that had no flexibility. Now I can enjoy the children, and as some have grown and left home, they tell me I am the best mother in the world. Now my goals are more attainable, and everyone is more comfortable.

MARILEE HORTON

*M*ost of us want children; we are not like that movie star who said that she refused to bring children into such a savage world as ours, to slave and sacrifice for them, and then see them destroyed in another world war. There aren't very many women who share her opinion. Most of us are like the childless Rachel of Old Testament days who cried out to her husband, "Give me children, or I'll die" (Genesis 30:1). Sure, when they come, and when at times they drive us nearly frantic, we are tempted to cry out that we'll die trying to take care of them, but we forget all that when they put their arms around our necks, or come running with a skinned knee. We want children, in spite of all the heartaches they bring with them.

DALE EVANS ROGERS

———— • • • ● • • • ————

Deborah Shaw Lewis, *Motherhood Stress*, 1989, 1992, Zondervan Publishing House, Grand Rapids, MI.

Margie M. Lewis, *The Hurting Parent,* © 1994 Zondervan Publishing House, Grand Rapids, MI

Anne Morrow Lindbergh, *Gift from the Sea*, © 1955, 1975, renewed 1983 by Anne Morrow Lindbergh. Reprinted by permission of Pantheon Books, a division of Random House, Inc.

Carole Mayhall, *When God Whispers*, by Carole Mayhall, © 1997, Used by permission of NavPress/Pinon Press. All rights reserved. For copies call 1-800-366-7788.

Kathi Mills, Barbara Johnson quoted in *Mommy Where Are You?*, © 1992, Harvest House Publishers, Eugene, OR.

Elisa Morgan, *NIV Mom's Devotional Bible*, 1996, Zondervan Publishing House, Grand Rapids, MI., *Mom to Mom*, 1996, Zondervan Publishing House, Grand Rapids, MI.

Elisa Morgan & Carol Kuykendall, *What Every Mom Needs*, 1995, Zondervan Publishing House, Grand Rapids, MI.

Robin Rice Morris, *"Heroes"* from Mothers At Home homepage.

Donna Otto, Taken From: *The Stay At Home Mom* © 1991, 1997 by Donna Otto, Published by Harvest House Publishers, Eugene, OR 97402. Used by permission.

Kathy Peel, *Do Plastic Surgeons Take VISA?*, Kathy Peel, © 1992, Word Publishing, Nashville, TN. All rights reserved.

Dale Evans Rogers, *Time Out, Ladies.* Fleming H. Revell, a division of Baker Book House Company, © 1966.

Hannah Whitall Smith, *The Christian's Secret of a Happy Life*, © 1942, Fleming H. Revell, Grand Rapids, MI.

Margaret B. Spiess, *Gather Me Together, Lord*, Baker Book House Company, © 1982.

———— • • • ● • • • ————